Obamacare Explained

Ronald Haines

Liability Disclaimer

By reading this book, you assume all risks associated with using the advice given, with a full understanding that you, solely, are responsible for anything that may occur as a result of putting this information into action in any way, and regardless of your interpretation of the advice.

Terms of Use

You are given a non-transferable, "personal use" license to this book. You cannot make copies of it to share with other individuals.

Obamacare Explained

Table of Contents

Introduction to Obamacare

Obamacare, or the Affordable Care Act, is the most sweeping piece of social legislation in America since the passing of Medicare and Medicaid in 1965 and it is going to have an impact on the scale of the 1978 amendment to the Internal Revenue Code which forever changed American workers' retirement benefits with the creation of 401k plans. A huge shift in the way Americans under the age of 65 pay for their health benefits starts in 2014 and experts are predicting that over 100 million American workers will no longer receive health insurance through their employers within two years. Americans are about to take on the responsibility for their own health insurance, just as they now do for their retirement.

Obamacare is now the law of the land; are you ready for it? This book contains the answers to your questions in simple, straight to the point, easy to understand English. Inside you will find concise answers to how health insurance is going to change and what those changes mean to you. When finished with this short read you will have a comprehensive knowledge of how this law affects you, what your options are and things you can do right now that will save you money in 2014.

What you will not find in this book is theory, rationale or politics. What you need are the facts provided here, everything else is academic.

Do you know what percentage of your income the government defines as "affordable" coverage?

Will you be eligible for government subsidies to help you pay for it?

Why most Americans under 65 will not be able to keep what they have?

Find the answers in this book: a must read for every American under the age of 65.

Background

Impact to Date

Obamacare was signed into law on March 23, 2010 and has been systematically being implemented since then and several benefit mandates are already in place. On September 23, 2010, the law stated that all new plans must provide that:

(1) Children can stay on their parents plan until age 26

(2) Preventive care, including mammograms and colonoscopies must be provided at no cost to the insured

(3) Lifetime dollar limits on services received were eliminated

(4) Children under the age of 19 cannot be refused coverage due to a pre-existing condition.

Then on August 1, 2012, all new plans were required to provide:

(5) Women's contraceptive coverage at no cost.

2014

The biggest impact takes place on January 1, 2014 when Obamacare mandates that every American will be required by law to have health insurance and that nobody can be denied a health insurance policy by an insurer. Five states, Massachusetts, Maine, New York, New Jersey and Vermont, already have this Guaranteed Issue law on the books so people who live there are already paying higher premiums than the rest of the country so the rate impact for them from this provision will be minimal at most.

A New Insurance Marketplace

In terms of where you get your insurance, Obamacare is not going to replace the current markets, but it will provide another option called Public (or Government) Exchanges. Public exchanges are simply marketplaces where you can compare different plan offerings from different insurance companies. Many people will enjoy the convenience of shopping the exchanges online or purchasing their health insurance over the telephone, while others will want to have their options explained on a face to face basis by a Navigator, a person who has been trained and authorized to do so.

Mandates

Obamacare also mandates that certain benefits, called Essential Health Benefits (EHBs), be included in every health plan, and it eliminates insurance company underwriting, which means everyone of the same age living in the same geographical area will pay the same rate for the same plan. This is called Community Rating. Seven states already have community rating, namely the above mentioned states plus Oregon and Washington.

Changes in Rating

The federal law also reduces the amount of disparity in rates between ages so that a 64 year old will only pay 3 times as much as a 19 year old. Some of the states mentioned above already have laws in place that are stronger than this, however, and in New York and for certain plans in Vermont age and gender rating is illegal.

Cost of Health Insurance

The overall cost of health insurance in America is obviously going to increase under Obamacare for the simple reason that there are going to be more claims for the insurance companies to pay out. These claims will be coming from two sources. First, the law requires new benefits that previously may not have been included in health insurance plans, so insurance will have to start covering them and, second, there will be an influx of people into the pool who were previously excluded due to health conditions. Insurance company profits were capped by Obamacare in January 2011 when the law required them to spend at least 85% of the premium collected from large companies and 80% of the premium from individuals and small companies to be spent on claims, so the costs for these additional claims are simply going to be passed through.

Cost Subsidies

A higher premium for health insurance doesn't necessarily mean that the amount you are going to pay will increase, however. The majority of Americans who buy health insurance on their own are going to qualify for subsidies. If you make less than 400% of the federal poverty level you may be eligible for government assistance to help you pay for your plan.

Medicare and Medicaid

This book is written for individuals, families and sole proprietors who are not on one of the government health programs: Medicare (health insurance for Americans over the age of 65 or who have certain disabilities) or Medicaid (health insurance for individuals and families with low income). Medicare and Medicaid currently cover 100 million Americans and it was originally expected that up to an additional 20 million of the 40 million people who are currently uninsured would be added to the Medicaid roles. Obamacare intended to expand Medicaid eligibility to all Americans from ages 19 to 64 with income up to 133% of the federal poverty level starting in 2014. However, in June, 2012, the Supreme Court ruled that Medicaid expansion would be up to each state to decide. Clearly, a large group of the currently uninsured will still be added to the Medicaid roles and the remainder of the uninsured will be included into the general insurance pool via the exchanges.

Grandfathered Plans

If you have health insurance that has not changed since before Obamacare was signed into law in March 23, 2010, you have a grandfathered plan and you may have the option to keep the plan you have or change to one of the new insurance plans which include the new benefits. However, since many of the provisions of Obamacare do not apply to grandfathered plans, chances are good that keeping a grandfathered plan may be your least expensive alternative for health insurance going forward.

How you'll be Getting Health Insurance

The law is that you must have insurance, so if you are not on Medicare or Medicaid or are not covered under a grandfathered plan there are three ways to go about getting it. You still have the choice not to have insurance, but under the new law you will then be subject to a penalty.

No matter where you get your health insurance, the new plans available to you will fall into one of 4 standardized categories, all of which are required to meet a minimum benefit level. This standardization will make it easy to compare plans offered by different insurance companies because they will basically be the same benefit-wise, so you can make your decisions based on providers in the insurance company networks, cost of the plan and perhaps the availability of additional or optional benefits.

Individual Market

The current market for purchasing individual and family health insurance plans is not going away, but the plans being offered beginning in 2014 will have to at least meet the standardized criteria. This means that if you currently buy your health insurance on your own, unless you have made no changes to it since before March, 2010, you are probably not going to be able to keep what you have now.

These new plan offerings will most likely be bundled under private (not government) exchanges and may be attractive by offering more options and fewer forms to complete, but people who purchase from private exchanges will not be eligible for government subsidies.

Public (Government) Exchanges

Unlike Medicare and Medicaid, this is not a government provided health insurance program. Plans in the public exchanges will be available from the same insurance companies you are familiar with who have received government approval to include their plans in the product offerings. Some states will be operating their own exchanges while others will be operated by the federal government.

Employer Sponsored Health Insurance

The majority of Americans under the age of 65 currently receive their health insurance through their employer, but that may change as employers consider their options under the new law. Many employers, especially those with less than 50 employees, are expected to make dramatic changes in their benefit offerings over the next few years. Currently, there are over 150 million people covered through employer group plans in the United States but by some estimates that number is expected to drop to 20 million within the next two years with the majority of employees shifting from group coverage to purchasing individual and family coverage through the exchanges.

Some employers will continue to offer group coverage. Those who have grandfathered plans will have the option to continue with what they have but most employers will be required to make significant changes. As an employee you may be offered anything from a single option to a selection of plans where the employer pays a fixed amount and you pay the difference based on your election. Affordability will be based on the lowest cost plan in such an offering.

Some employers may offer reimbursement accounts which provide you with a fixed dollar amount which you can use to buy any plan you like from the public or private exchanges. This is called a Defined Contribution plan and takes the employer out of the decision making in terms of the benefit; he just provides a certain contribution to help you pay for it. This will be an attractive option to many small employers because the only reason they provided health insurance in the past was to ensure that all of their employees, some of whom may not have been eligible for insurance in the individual market due to health conditions, had coverage. Now that nobody can be denied coverage through the exchanges this reason no longer exists.

Other employers will simply be dropping their health insurance altogether. There is no requirement under the law for employers with less than 50 employees to offer coverage, so they are not subject to any penalties if they decide to no longer offer it. And while companies with 50 or more employees are required to offer coverage or pay a penalty, the cost of the penalties may be much lower than the cost of providing insurance coverage that meets the new requirements.

As a practical matter, however, certain companies that currently do offer health benefits, especially larger employers and those requiring special skills will most likely continue to do so in some form as a means of attracting and retaining employees.

No Coverage

Not all Americans who are currently uninsured are living below the poverty level; many people who can afford health insurance simply choose not to buy it. These include sole proprietors who do not want to pay what they consider to be high insurance premiums and the "young and invincible" population who may or may not have it available to them through their employers. A major concern is that many of these, especially the "young and invincible" who currently make up 48% of the uninsured population, may continue to remain uninsured because the penalties are significantly less than the cost of insurance. If this does happen it will remove many healthy people from the expected insurance pool and drive up the overall cost of insurance.

Will Health Insurance be Affordable

Insurance rates are going to increase for the majority of Americans, but by being subsidized either by the government or an employer most people will not be paying that entire cost. By no longer having rates for health insurance based on medical underwriting, costs are simply going to be averaged across the board with the result being that the cost of insurance will go up the most for the healthy and potentially down for the unhealthy. This is just simple mathematics.

Also, with the maximum ratio of highest to lowest cost being 3 times based on age (lower or not at all in some states as mentioned previously), insurance rates for most older people will come down and for younger people will go up.

These two facts may end up further incentivizing the "young and invincible" population not to participate, and since these are the people who would be expected to have very few claims, their premiums would have helped to offset the costs of the higher utilizing people. If this happens in any great numbers the insurance companies will have to, perhaps dramatically, raise their premiums in the future in order to remain solvent.

The actual name for Obamacare is the Affordable Care Act and it defines affordable care as costing 9.5% of your income. There is no free ride here, but those who have low incomes may be eligible for subsidies on a sliding scale if they buy their health insurance through the public exchanges.

Subsidies

Anyone with income between 133% and 400% of the federal poverty level who purchases health insurance through a public exchange may be eligible for subsidies. The approximate ranges are:

Income for an individual from $14,850 to $44,680
Income for a husband and wife $19,560 to $58,840
Income for a family of four from $30,650 to $92,200

There will be a separate application, available online, to complete to determine if you and your family quality for a government subsidy.

For people who earn up to 250% of the federal poverty level there will also be cost-sharing help available. These are additional subsidies to help reduce the overall out of pocket maximums and will be applied against the silver level plans only. They will most likely take the form of a richer plan available only to those eligible.

Everyone will be able to purchase insurance through the public exchanges but not everyone will be eligible for a subsidy, even if their income is less than 400% of the federal poverty level. If your employer offers you health insurance that meets the minimum essential coverage and it is considered affordable for you, you will not be eligible for a subsidy, even if you decline your employer's plan.

Individual Market, or Private Exchanges

There will be no government subsidies for people who buy from private exchanges, but there may be more plan options available. The buyers in this group will most likely consist of people:

Who make over 400% of the federal poverty level and/or would like more choices

Who do not wish to take employer group coverage or want a lower cost for their dependent coverage than is available through the group (takes group employee coverage and buys coverage for dependents separately) Who don't want to bother with the additional forms associated with the government exchanges and are not concerned with receiving a subsidy

Public (Government) Exchanges

Since affordable has been defined as 9.5% of your income, if you earn less than 400% of the federal poverty level that is what you can expect to pay because there will be subsidies available to you to pay for the rest of the actual cost of your insurance premium. However, if your employer offers a qualified plan that would cost you less than 9.5% of your pay and you don't take it, you will not be eligible for an exchange subsidy. The subsidies are only available to people who have no other qualified option.

You do not need to qualify for a subsidy to be able to purchase from the public exchanges; they will be available to everyone.

Employer Sponsored

Group insurance that meets the minimum essential coverage criteria and costs the employee no more than 9.5% of his/her income is considered a qualified plan. In order to remain in compliance, employee pay is one of the calculations employers will have to take into consideration when determining contributions for health insurance. Employers have no responsibility to pay for dependent coverage, however, and the 9.5% is calculated only against the cost for a single employee. As of the time of this writing (April, 2013), if an employee declines dependent coverage in a qualified group plan then those dependents will not be eligible for government subsidies in a public exchange.

No coverage

The penalties for those who decide not to take health insurance are:

In 2014, the greater of $95 or 1% of taxable income
In 2015, the greater of $325 or 2% of taxable income
In 2016, the greater of $695 or 2.5% of taxable income

To be adjusted annually thereafter.

Increased Taxes for Higher Earners

One of the ways to help fund Obamacare was to increase taxes on people who earn in excess of $200,000/year for a single and $250,000/year for a family. These two laws went into effect in January, 2013:

Tax on high earners of a 0.9% increase in Medicare tax on earnings in excess of $200,000 single and $250,000 married

Tax on unearned income of 3.8% in excess of $200,000 single and $250,000 married

Coverage: Essential Health Benefits

The Essential Health Benefits (EHBs) are a set of basic coverage requirements that all plans must provide but there will be state to state differences because each state is able to set their own benchmark plan which will define their minimal coverage for each of the categories. This base coverage, then, may be richer in some states than in others.

There will be no annual or lifetime dollar limit on EHBs. There are 10 EHB categories that all plans must provide coverage in:

1. Ambulatory patient services
2. Emergency services
3. Hospitalization
4. Maternity and newborn care
5. Mental health and substance use disorder services
6. Prescription drugs
7. Rehabilitative and habilitative services and devices
8. Laboratory services
9. Preventive and wellness services and chronic disease

management

10. Pediatric services, including oral and vision care

While many health insurance plans that currently exist do provide a certain degree of coverage in most of these areas, the new rules will require much more standardization between them.

One of the most notable expansions in coverage for many states is in the area of mental health and substance abuse, which will also have to include behavioral health treatment.

New to most health plans is the requirement that pediatric dental and vision must be a covered benefit. This will be accomplished by either embedding these benefits into a health plan or else having stand-alone dental/vision plans in the exchanges. Adult dental and vision are not included in the EHBs.

Types of Plans

The differences in plans, therefore, will not be about what services are covered, that will be determined by the state benchmarks and the EHBs, but what the cost sharing of those services under each of the plans will be until a maximum out of pocket amount has been reached. The maximum out of pocket in 2014 is expected to be $6,350 for one person and $12,700 for a family and will be adjusted annually in future years. These out of pocket costs will apply to everybody, the subsidies for most Americans will only help with the cost of the premiums. However, those with an income of less than 250% of the federal poverty level will be eligible to receive additional help to pay for these out of pocket costs.

Obamacare calls for four tiers of cost sharing which are being referred to as the Metal Levels:

The Platinum plans must meet a 90% actuarial value
The Gold plans must meet an 80% actuarial value
The Silver plans must meet a 70% actuarial value
The Bronze plans must meet a 60% actuarial value

Actuarial value refers to the amount the insurance company will pay and the individual insured will then pay the remainder and will most likely be presented in the familiar deductible and coinsurance format, but for our purposes that is just behind the scenes calculations. What matters, and the thing to keep in mind is that the bronze plans will have the lowest premiums but the highest out of pocket costs (highest deductibles and percentage coinsurance) and the platinum plans will have the highest premiums but the lowest out of pocket costs. However, they will all have the same maximum out of pocket limits.

Enrolling in a Plan

For the public exchanges the initial open enrollment will be from October, 2013 to the end of March 2014, with the first effective month being January, 2014. Open enrollment will then happen annually for a 45 day period in the last quarter of each year. This will be the time in which you will be able to join a plan or switch from one plan to another. While open enrollment for public exchanges will be specified, open enrollments for the private exchanges may end up being quite different for each state. Some states already have defined open enrollment periods which may or may not remain. For example:

New York and Maine currently require year round open enrollment.

Virginia and Ohio have year round open enrollment plans for people who do not otherwise have access to coverage.

California requires an open enrollment period for people

who have coverage to move to an equal or lesser plan if they have been covered for at least 18 continuous months.

Wisconsin allows people who have insurance to move to less rich coverage at renewal.

Special open enrollment periods exist in California, Colorado, Georgia, Kentucky, Indiana and Missouri for children only.

Applying for a Subsidy

The amount of time needed to complete an application to apply for a subsidy is estimated to be half an hour online or forty five minutes for a paper application. Once you have submitted your application to the public exchange, they will send the information to the Data Services Hub who will forward it to several federal agencies for verification:

Social Security to check birth records
Internal Revenue Service for income verification
Homeland Security to verify immigration status

These federal agencies will then send the verified information back to the hub, which will forward the results back to the exchange. The exchange will notify the applicant as to whether they qualify for a subsidy.

Money Saving Tips

Here are some things you can do before open enrollment which have the potential to save you a lot of money in 2014.

Play a Safety

If you purchase your own health insurance check with your insurance carrier as soon as possible to find out if your current plan will be changing in January or will go until your annual renewal before it changes. If you have until your annual renewal and it is sometime during 2014 you will be able to compare options during open enrollment and if what you have is cheaper you can at least keep it until renewal.

If you are in good health and live in a state that will still be underwriting new policies until 2014 you should consider shopping around. Some insurance carriers are guaranteeing current plans and rates through the end of 2014 and if those rates look good it might be worth making a switch now. By playing a safety like this you'll be in a position to decide to take one of the new plans or keep what you have for another year. It is possible that changes or tweaks may be made to the law after it is implemented in January, 2014 and this strategy may enable you to stay with this plan while changes are being put in place.

Check with your Employer

If you work for a company which has less than 50 employees that company is not subject to penalties regarding their health insurance plan. But, if they do offer a qualified plan it will eliminate your chance at subsidies if you wish to purchase coverage which might otherwise be available at a lower cost to you and your family through an exchange. You would be turned down for a subsidy even if you were to decline company coverage because a qualified plan was available to you.

Here are two strategies a small employer might adopt to give you and him the best of both worlds.

Not Affordable Strategy

If a small employer with less than 50 employees offers a plan that is 'not affordable' he would have no penalty, but you could get a subsidy. Not affordable is defined as the employee contribution to the employee-only health insurance (dependent coverage is not part of the calculation) costing more than 9.5% of salary. So, if your employer set the employee only contribution high enough where it would exceed 9.5% of your pay, you could then purchase federally subsidized coverage through the exchange. Eligibility for a subsidy is considered on an individual basis so it is possible that lower paid employees may qualify whereas a higher paid employee at the same company who would have to pay the same contribution would not. It all depends upon the employee's cost of individual employee coverage as a percentage of their income.

Health Reimbursement Allowance

This works whether you have dependents or not. Ask your employer to consider implementing a health reimbursement allowance, or HRA. With this type of a plan your company does not offer an insurance plan and instead gives a set dollar amount which you could use to purchase your own health insurance in the exchanges.

About The Author

Ronald Haines is the president of HCI Employee Benefits, an employee benefits brokerage in Ohio serving individuals, small businesses and seniors. For more than 20 years, Ronald's clients have benefited from his expertise as a benefits broker and his ability to explain complex matters in easy to understand, simple English.

This book deals with Obamacare in the same manner. Here you will find concise answers about how health insurance is going to change, what it means to you and what your options are. When finished with this short read you will have a comprehensive knowledge of how this law affects you, what your options are and things you can do right now that will save you money in 2014.

Made in the USA
Charleston, SC
24 December 2013